THE ART OF MANIFESTATION ESSENTIALS FOR BLACK WOMEN

A MENTAL HEALTH WORKBOOK TO CREATING YOUR DREAMS, HARNESSING YOUR INNER STRENGTH AND UNCOVERING YOUR TRUE POTENTIAL

MINDSET MASTERY AND SELF-CARE FOR BLACK WOMEN

JADA AMARI

ISBN: 978-1-953149-49-7

Published by: Jada Amari
© Copyright 2023 - All rights reserved.

CONTENTS

Free Gifts   v

Introduction   vii

1. The Secret to Unlocking Your Dreams   1
2. Discovering Your Hidden Superpower   11
3. Building the Life You Deserve   21
   Spread Black Women's Empowerment   31
4. Breaking Free from Self-Sabotage   33
5. The Key to Unlocking Your Best Self   43
6. One Daily Habit for Transforming Your Life   55

Conclusion   65
References   69

Are you tired of the endless diet culture and ready to cultivate a more positive and mindful relationship with food?

This comprehensive guide offers tips, strategies, and exercises for practicing mindful eating to promote physical and emotional health.

From healthy recipes to nutritional advice, you'll find everything you need to nourish your body and mind with intention and care.

Say goodbye to mindless snacking and hello to a more balanced and positive relationship with food.

- Unleash the Hidden Potential Within You and Unlock the Key to Abundance!
- Discover the Secrets to Manifesting the Life You Deserve Through the Power of the Universe.
- Experience a Life of Limitless Opportunities and Overcome Your Deepest Fears and Doubts.
- Open the Door to Unlimited Happiness, Success, and Abundance with These Powerful Tips and Techniques!

INTRODUCTION

"Black women are magic. Period." - Unknown

We are queens, warriors, innovators, and trailblazers. We have overcome adversity, broken barriers, and made history. But sometimes, even the strongest among us need a little extra help, a little extra magic, to reach our full potential. And that's where I come in.

My name is Jada Amari, and I'm a manifestation expert. I help Black women like you harness the power of manifestation to create the life of your dreams. You may be wondering what manifestation is and how it can help you. Well, let me tell you, it's not some magical woo-woo that only works for certain people. Manifestation is a real, practical, and effective way to transform your life. And I'm here to show you how.

As a Black woman myself, I understand the unique challenges and opportunities that we face in pursuing our dreams. From societal barriers to self-doubt, we have a lot to overcome. But I truly believe that we are unstoppable when we tap into our inner strength and harness the power of manifestation.

So, why am I credible to teach you about manifestation? Well, it all started with my own personal journey. I was once a struggling college student, unsure of my path and purpose. But through my own manifestation practice, I was able to transform my life and become a successful entrepreneur, speaker, and author.

But it's not just my own journey that makes me credible. I've also worked with countless Black women over the years, helping them achieve their goals and manifest their dreams. I've seen firsthand the incredible transformations that can occur when we tap into our inner strength and harness the power of manifestation.

This book is not just about me or my journey, though. It's about you and your journey. The Art of Manifestation Essentials for Black Women is a guide specifically tailored for Black women who want to create the life they desire. In this book, you will discover the key principles of manifestation and how they apply to Black women. You will learn simple yet effective techniques to cultivate self-awareness and overcome limiting beliefs. You will discover the importance of self-care, gratitude, and visualization in manifesting your dreams. And much more!

But most importantly, you will learn how to harness your inner strength and uncover your true potential. That's the real magic of manifestation—it's not about changing the world around you, it's about changing yourself from within.

Let's start by addressing the elephant in the room—the fact that Black women face unique challenges that often make it difficult to pursue our dreams. Society has put us in a box, telling us what we can and can't do, what we should and shouldn't be. But I'm here to tell you that you can break out of that box and become whatever you want to be. Manifestation is the key to unlocking your full potential and creating the life you desire.

The first step to manifestation is understanding what it is and how it works. At its core, manifestation is the process of bringing your thoughts and desires into reality. It's about aligning your thoughts, emotions, and actions with your goals and desires. The principles of manifestation are based on the law of attraction, which states that like attracts like. In other words, the energy you put out into the universe is the energy you attract back to you.

Now, you may be thinking, "That sounds great, but how does it work in real life?" That's where the rest of this book comes in. We'll be diving deep into the specific techniques and strategies you can use to harness the power of manifestation and create the life you desire. But before we get into all that, let's talk about why manifestation is particularly important for Black women.

As I mentioned earlier, Black women face unique challenges in pursuing our dreams. We often have to navigate a world that was not designed with us in mind. We have to fight against systemic racism, sexism, and other forms of discrimination that hold us back. And sometimes, we even have to fight against our own self-doubt and limiting beliefs.

That's why manifestation is so important for Black women. It's a way for us to take control of our lives and create the reality we desire, despite the challenges we face. When we harness the power of manifestation, we tap into our own inner strength and become unstoppable.

But I want to be clear—manifestation is not a quick fix or a magic solution. It's a practice that requires dedication, patience, and perseverance. It's about making a commitment to yourself and your goals and working every day to align your thoughts, emotions, and actions with your desires.

That's why I wrote this book—to give Black women the tools and strategies they need to grasp the art of manifestation. In the following chapters, we'll be diving deep into the key principles of manifestation and how they apply specifically to Black women. We'll explore the importance of connecting with your inner strength, defining your dreams and goals, overcoming limiting beliefs, cultivating self-awareness, and much more.

But before we get into all that, I want to take a moment to acknowledge the pain and struggles that Black women face every day. I know that life can be hard, and sometimes it can feel like the odds are stacked against us. But I want you to know that you are not alone. You are part of a community of strong, powerful, and resilient Black women who are working every day to create the lives they desire.

And that's why I wrote this book. I want to empower Black women to take control of their lives and create the reality they desire. I want to help you tap into your own inner magic and become the best version of yourself.

So, my fellow Black queens, are you ready to create the life of your dreams and unleash your full potential? If so, let's get started. The Art of Manifestation Essentials for Black Women is the guide you need to make it happen.

Let's dive in and make some magic!

THE SECRET TO UNLOCKING YOUR DREAMS

"If you have a dream, don't just sit there. Gather courage to believe that you can succeed and leave no stone unturned to make it a reality." - Dr. Roopleen

*H*ey there, girl! I hope you're ready to embark on an amazing journey to transform your life. This first chapter is all about understanding the art of manifestation. It's a powerful tool that can help you create the life of your dreams, and I'm here to show you how.

In this chapter, we'll be covering the basic principles of manifestation and how they apply specifically to Black women. We'll be talking about the role of mindset and intention in manifestation, and the power of manifestation in transforming your life.

Now, I know this might all sound a little out there or confusing, but stick with me. Manifestation is all about aligning your thoughts, emotions, and actions with your goals and desires. It's about creating a mindset of abundance and positivity that allows you to attract the things you want in life.

Let's begin!

WHAT IS MANIFESTATION?

First, let's talk about the basic principles of manifestation. At its core, manifestation is about bringing your dreams and desires into reality by focusing your thoughts and energy on them. It's about tapping into the power of the universe and aligning yourself with the things you want to manifest. Sounds simple, right? It is, but it requires a little bit of work on your part.

One of the fundamental principles of manifestation is the law of attraction. The law of attraction is the idea that like attracts like. So, if you want to manifest something, you need to focus on the positive aspects of it and believe that it's already yours. For example, if you want a promotion at work, focus on the positive aspects of the promotion, such as the increased salary, the added responsibility, and the opportunities for growth. Visualize yourself in that new position, feel the joy and excitement, and trust that it's already on its way to you.

Another key principle of manifestation is the power of visualization. Visualization is the practice of creating a mental image of what you want to manifest. It's a powerful tool that helps you to focus your thoughts and energy on your desires. Visualization can be as simple as closing your eyes and imagining yourself living your dream life. The more you visualize, the more real it becomes to you, and the easier it is to manifest it into your reality.

To manifest your desires successfully, you need to align your thoughts, beliefs, and actions with your intentions. This means that you need to believe that what you want is possible, and you need to take action towards it. You can't just sit on the couch and expect your dreams to fall into your lap. You need to take inspired action and work towards your goals.

Now, I know what some of you may be thinking. "Jada, this all sounds great, but it's not that easy. Life gets in the way, and things don't always go as planned." I hear you, sis, but that's where the power of perseverance comes in. Perseverance is the willingness to keep going, even when things get tough. It's the determination to push through obstacles and keep your eye on the prize. It's the key to manifesting your dreams, no matter what challenges come your way.

POSITIVE MINDSET AND SETTING CLEAR INTENTIONS

At its core, manifestation is about bringing your dreams and desires into reality through the power of your thoughts, beliefs, and actions. It's about taking control of your life and creating the future you want, rather than just letting life happen to you.

But in order to truly manifest your dreams, you need to start with the right mindset. This means having a positive attitude and a belief in yourself and your abilities. You must truly believe that you can achieve your goals and that you deserve to have the life you want.

A positive mindset is not just about thinking happy thoughts—it's about understanding the power of your thoughts and the impact they have on your life. When you focus on negative thoughts and self-doubt, you create a negative energy that can hold you back from achieving your goals. But when you focus on positive thoughts and beliefs, you create a powerful energy that can help you manifest your dreams with ease.

In addition to a positive mindset, it's important to set clear intentions for what you want to manifest. This means getting specific about your goals and being clear about what you want to achieve. The more specific you are, the easier it will be to create a clear vision for your future and to take action towards your goals.

When setting intentions, it's also important to focus on the present moment. This means staying focused on what you want to achieve now, rather than worrying about the past or future. When you focus on the present, you can create a powerful energy that will help you manifest your goals with ease.

Another key aspect of manifestation is taking action towards your goals. This means taking concrete steps towards achieving what you want, rather than just hoping and wishing for it to happen. When you take action, you show the universe that you are serious about your goals, and you create momentum that can help you manifest your dreams faster.

It's important to stay open to receiving what you want. This means being open to new opportunities and ideas, and not getting too attached to a specific outcome. When you stay open and flexible, you can create a powerful energy that will attract the right people, circumstances, and opportunities to help you achieve your goals.

As a Black woman, it's especially important to harness this skill to overcome the unique challenges that we face and create the future we want.

THE UNIQUE CHALLENGES US BLACK WOMEN FACE

As Black women, we have faced many unique challenges in our journey towards manifesting our dreams. It is essential to acknowledge these challenges and turn them into opportunities that can help us unleash our full potential. Let's talk about some of the unique challenges that Black women face when it comes to manifestation and how to overcome them.

The first challenge we face is the lack of representation. Most of the books, movies, and other resources available on manifestation do not cater to the Black woman. As a result, we are left feeling like our dreams and aspirations are not valid or relevant. It is vital to acknowledge that we need to see ourselves in the stories we consume. The key is to find resources and mentors that resonate with our experiences and cultural backgrounds. Seek out and connect with other successful Black women who have manifested their dreams. By doing this, you can learn from their experiences and be inspired by their journeys.

Another challenge we face is the pressure to conform to society's expectations. As Black women, we are expected to fulfill certain roles and behave in specific ways that may not align with our authentic selves. This can be detrimental to our manifestation journey because it hinders us from tapping into our inner strength and true potential. The key is to let go of these societal expectations and create our paths. We need to embrace our unique qualities and let them guide us toward manifesting our dreams.

Self-doubt and limiting beliefs are another obstacle we face when it comes to manifestation. Society has programmed us to believe that we are not enough, that we do not have what it takes to achieve our dreams. As Black women, we are often told that we have to work twice as hard to get half as much, which can lead to self-doubt and limiting beliefs. The key is to recognize that these are just societal constructs and do not define us. We need to start affirming ourselves positively, changing our inner dialogue from negative to positive. By doing this, we can transform our limiting beliefs into empowering ones that will help us manifest our dreams.

We also face challenges when it comes to financial stability. Many of us come from backgrounds that did not have the financial resources to support our dreams. This lack of financial stability can make it challenging to manifest our dreams, as we may not have access to resources or the funds to pursue our goals. The key is to be resourceful and start small. We can start by investing in ourselves and our education, seeking out free or low-cost resources, and building our network. By taking small steps and being consistent, we can manifest our dreams despite the financial challenges we face.

INFLUENTIAL BLACK WOMEN

As a Black woman, it's important to know that manifestation is not only accessible to everyone, but it's also something that has been used by many of our sisters who have achieved great things. Let's explore some real-life examples of Black women who have used manifestation to achieve their goals.

First up is Oprah Winfrey, a household name who has used manifestation throughout her career. Oprah has spoken at length about the power of visualization, and how she used it to turn her dreams into a reality. From a young age, Oprah had a clear vision of the life she wanted to live, and through her determination and focus, she was able to manifest it into existence. Through visualization and positive affirmations, Oprah was able to create a life that not only fulfilled her own dreams but also inspired millions of others to do the same.

Another great example of a Black woman who has used manifestation is Beyoncé. As one of the most successful musicians in the world, Beyoncé has always been open about the importance of setting clear intentions and working towards your goals. Through hard work, discipline, and a strong belief in herself, Beyoncé has been able to manifest incredible success in her career. But it's not just her career that she has manifested. Beyoncé has also used manifestation to create a beautiful family and to maintain a healthy, happy lifestyle.

Next up is Ava DuVernay, a talented filmmaker who has used manifestation to achieve her dreams. Ava is known for her powerful and moving work, and it's clear that her success is a result of her unwavering belief in herself and her vision. Ava has spoken about how important it is to stay focused on your goals, even in the face of adversity. Through the power of manifestation, Ava has been able to create a career that is not only successful but also deeply fulfilling.

And let's not forget about Serena Williams, one of the greatest athletes of all time. Serena has been able to manifest incredible success through her unwavering focus, discipline, and belief in herself. She has spoken about the importance of visualization and positive affirmations, and how they have helped her to achieve her goals both on and off the court. Through the power of manifestation, Serena has been able to create a life that is not only successful but also deeply fulfilling.

These are just a few examples of Black women who have used manifestation to achieve their goals. But the truth is, there are countless others who have used this powerful tool to create the lives they want. From entrepreneurs and businesswomen to artists and activists, Black women are using manifestation to unlock their true potential and create a life that is both successful and fulfilling. You see? This stuff really does work!

SUMMARY, ACTION STEPS & EXERCISES:

- Spend some time visualizing your ideal life. What does it look like? How does it feel? What are you doing?
- Write down your goals and desires, and set clear intentions for how you want to achieve them.
- Start cultivating a positive mindset by practicing gratitude and affirmations.
- Be mindful of your thoughts and emotions, and try to shift any negative patterns.

I hope you found the first chapter insightful and informative.

We started by exploring the basic principles of manifestation, which can be a powerful tool for transforming your life. We talked about the law of attraction, which is the idea that like attracts like, and how it's essential to align your thoughts, emotions, and actions with your goals and desires in order to manifest them.

We also explored the power of visualization, which is a technique used by successful people to create mental images of their goals as if they have already achieved them. Visualization can help you to bring your desires into your reality by programming your subconscious mind to work towards your goals.

We discussed the importance of having a positive mindset and setting clear intentions, and how this can help you to overcome limiting beliefs that might be holding you back. We explored the concept of limiting beliefs and how they can manifest in different ways in our lives.

We then talked about the unique challenges and opportunities that Black women face when it comes to manifesting their dreams.

Finally, we touched on other successful Black women who have had a profound positive impact on their lives using the art of manifestation.

Now that you understand the basic principles of manifestation and how it can work for you, it's time to take the next step and connect with your inner strength.

As a Black woman, you already possess a great deal of inner strength, but sometimes it can be hard to access it when you need it most. That's where the next chapter comes in.

We'll be exploring techniques for tapping into your inner strength, the importance of self-awareness in accessing your inner strength, and how to use your inner strength to overcome challenges. We'll be discussing the power of meditation, journaling, and affirmations, and how they can help you connect with your inner strength on a deeper level. Trust me, sis, you've got this!

2

DISCOVERING YOUR HIDDEN SUPERPOWER

"Strong women don't have attitudes. They have standards." - Unknown

*G*irl, I hope you're feeling inspired and ready to tap into your inner strength because that's what we're going to be talking about in this chapter. As Black women, we know that we're strong, but sometimes it can be hard to access that strength when we need it most. That's why it's so important to cultivate a deep connection with our inner strength, so we can call on it whenever we need to.

In this chapter, we're going to be covering some techniques for tapping into your inner strength, the importance of self-awareness in accessing your inner strength, and how to use your inner strength to overcome challenges. By the end of this chapter, you'll have a clear understanding of what inner strength is, how to access it, and how to use it to overcome any obstacle that comes your way. So, let's get started.

WHAT IS INNER STRENGTH?

As Black women, we often face a variety of challenges that can be draining, overwhelming, and emotionally taxing. From societal pressures to economic instability, these challenges can take a toll on our mental, emotional, and physical well-being. That is why it is crucial for us to cultivate inner strength, which is the corner-stone of our ability to manifest our dreams.

Inner strength is the mental, emotional, and spiritual fortitude that resides within each of us. It is the courage, resilience, and determination that enables us to overcome the obstacles we face and move towards our goals. Inner strength comes from a place of self-awareness, self-love, and self-respect. It is about being grounded in who we are and what we stand for, even when the world tries to tell us otherwise

For Black women, cultivating inner strength is vital because we face unique challenges that can be incredibly taxing on our sense of self. These challenges range from societal expectations and stereotypes to the lack of representation and financial instability. Inner strength helps us rise above these challenges by giving us the tools to stay centered, focused, and motivated.

Inner strength also helps us to tap into our true potential. When we have a strong sense of inner strength, we are more likely to take risks, pursue our dreams, and speak our truth. We are more resilient when things don't go as planned, and we are better equipped to bounce back from setbacks. Inner strength helps us stay true to ourselves and our purpose, even in the face of adversity.

To cultivate inner strength, we need to start by nurturing our relationship with ourselves. This means taking care of our mental, emotional, and physical well-being. It means engaging in self-care practices like meditation, exercise, and therapy. It means setting healthy boundaries and learning to say no when necessary. It means surrounding ourselves with people who lift us up and support us.

We also need to learn to embrace our unique qualities and strengths. We need to stop comparing ourselves to others and recognize that our journey is unique. It means acknowledging our successes and celebrating our wins, no matter how small they may be.

TECHNIQUES FOR TAPPING INTO YOUR INNER STRENGTH

As Black women, we have an incredible inner strength that we often overlook. In our daily lives, we juggle multiple roles, including motherhood, career, relationships, and personal growth. It's no wonder that sometimes we feel drained and disconnected from our inner selves. However, it's essential to tap into our inner strength regularly to achieve our goals and manifest our dreams. In this article, I will be sharing practical techniques for connecting with your inner strength, including meditation, journaling, and affirmations.

Meditation

Meditation is a powerful technique for tapping into your inner strength. It involves sitting in silence, focusing on your breath, and observing your thoughts without judgment. Meditation helps you to quiet the noise in your mind, reduces stress, and promotes inner peace. With regular meditation practice, you can cultivate a deep sense of inner strength and resilience.

To get started, find a quiet space where you won't be disturbed. Sit comfortably with your back straight, close your eyes, and focus on your breath. Start by taking deep breaths in through your nose and out through your mouth. As you breathe, focus your attention on your breath and observe the thoughts that come up without judgment. Don't try to push your thoughts away, simply observe them and bring your attention back to your breath. Start with five minutes and gradually increase the time as you get comfortable with the practice.

Journaling

Journaling is another powerful technique for connecting with your inner strength. It involves writing down your thoughts, feelings, and experiences on paper. Journaling helps you to clarify your thoughts, process your emotions, and gain a deeper understanding of yourself. With regular journaling practice, you can tap into your inner strength and gain clarity on your goals and dreams.

To get started, find a journal that resonates with you. Set aside some time each day to write down your thoughts and experiences. Start with a prompt, such as "What am I grateful for today?" or "What are my goals for the week?" Write down whatever comes to mind, without worrying about grammar or spelling. The key is to let your thoughts flow freely without judgment.

Affirmations

Affirmations are positive statements that you repeat to yourself to reprogram your subconscious mind. Affirmations can help you to cultivate a positive mindset, overcome self-doubt, and tap into your inner strength. With regular affirmation practice, you can train your mind to focus on positive thoughts and beliefs, which can help you to manifest your dreams.

To get started, create a list of positive affirmations that resonate with you. For example, "I am worthy of love and success" or "I am capable of achieving my goals." Repeat your affirmations to yourself daily, preferably in front of a mirror. Say them with conviction and believe in them. You can also write them down and place them where you can see them daily, such as on your fridge or in your workspace.

Tapping into your inner strength is essential for manifesting your dreams and achieving your goals. By incorporating techniques such as meditation, journaling, and affirmations into your daily routine, you can cultivate a deeper sense of self-awareness and inner strength. Remember that it takes practice and consistency to develop these habits, so be patient with yourself and enjoy the journey. With time, you will see the transformational impact of tapping into your inner strength.

THE IMPORTANCE OF SELF-AWARENESS IN ACCESSING YOUR INNER STRENGTH

It's time to cultivate some self-awareness! As Black women, we are often so busy juggling multiple roles that we forget to check in with ourselves. That's why cultivating self-awareness is essential to tap into our inner strength and manifest our dreams.

Self-awareness also helps you to identify your limiting beliefs and negative self-talk. When you are aware of these thoughts, you can challenge them and reframe them into more positive and empowering beliefs. By doing this, you can build your confidence and self-esteem, which is essential for accessing your inner strength.

Now, you may be wondering, "How can I cultivate more self-awareness in my life?" Well, I've got you covered! Here are some practical tips to get you started:

Self-reflection

The first step is to make time for self-reflection. This means taking some time out each day to check in with yourself and reflect on your thoughts and emotions. You can do this through meditation, journaling, or simply taking a few minutes to sit in silence and be present with yourself.

Self-observation

The second step is to practice self-observation. This means observing your thoughts, feelings, and behaviors without judgment. When you observe yourself in this way, you can start to identify patterns and triggers that impact your life. You can also start to notice your limiting beliefs and negative self-talk and begin to challenge them.

Feedback

The third step is to seek feedback from others. This means asking your friends, family, or coworkers for feedback on your strengths and areas for improvement. This feedback can help you to identify blind spots and gain a different perspective on yourself.

Open to change

The fourth step is to be open to change. This means being willing to change and grow. When you identify areas for improvement, be open to making changes in your life. This may involve stepping out of your comfort zone and taking risks, but it's essential for personal growth and accessing your inner strength.

By cultivating self-awareness through self-reflection, self-observation, seeking feedback from others, and being open to change, you can gain a deeper understanding of yourself and your potential. Remember that self-awareness is a journey, not a destination. It takes time, patience, and consistency to develop this skill. But with practice, you can tap into your inner strength and create the life you desire.

OVERCOMING CHALLENGES USING YOUR INNER STRENGTH

We often face challenges on our journey to manifesting our dreams. These challenges can range from self-doubt, societal expectations, financial instability, and much more.

However, we have an incredible inner strength that we can draw upon to overcome these obstacles and achieve our goals.

You are a strong, capable, and powerful woman who can achieve anything you set your mind to. The road may be bumpy, and you may face challenges, but with your inner strength, you can overcome anything.

So, let's get started on how to use your inner strength to overcome challenges.

Cultivate a positive mindset

The first thing you need to do is cultivate a positive mindset. I know this may sound cheesy, but your mindset is everything. You need to believe that you can achieve your dreams and that you have the power to overcome any obstacle. When you have a positive mindset, you are more likely to take action towards your goals and overcome challenges with ease.

Set clear and realistic goals

The second thing you need to do is set clear and realistic goals. It's essential to have a clear vision of what you want to achieve. When you have a goal in mind, it's easier to tap into your inner strength and take action towards it. Make sure your goals align with your values and that they are achievable. Break your goals down into smaller steps, and celebrate each milestone you achieve. Remember, small wins lead to big wins.

Take action towards your goals

The third thing you need to do is take action towards your goals, even when it's hard. This means stepping out of your comfort zone and taking risks. It also means being persistent and consistent in your efforts. When you take action towards your goals, you are showing yourself that you are capable of achieving your dreams. You are building your inner strength and resilience with each step you take.

Surround yourself with positive and supportive people
You need to have a tribe of people who believe in you and support your dreams. Seek out mentors and role models who have achieved success in the areas that you aspire to. Their stories can inspire you and give you the motivation you need to keep going.

Embrace failure and learn from it

Failure is not a bad thing. It's an opportunity for growth and learning. When you fail, reflect on what went wrong and what you can do differently next time. Use this information to adjust your approach and keep moving forward. Remember, failure is just a temporary setback. It doesn't define you, so don't let it stop you from manifesting your dreams.

Using your inner strength to overcome challenges is essential for manifesting your dreams. Cultivate a positive mindset, set clear and realistic goals, take action towards your goals, surround yourself with positive and supportive people, and embrace failure as an opportunity for growth.

SUMMARY, ACTION STEPS & EXERCISES:

- Take 10 minutes each day to meditate and connect with your inner strength.
- Start a journal and write down your thoughts and feelings to cultivate more self-awareness.
- Use positive affirmations to strengthen your inner dialogue and access your inner strength.
- Practice using your inner strength to overcome small challenges in your daily life.

* * *

As Black women, we know that we're strong, but sometimes it can be hard to access that strength when we need it most. That's why cultivating a deep connection with our inner strength is so important.

In this chapter, we discussed practical techniques for connecting with your inner strength, including meditation, journaling, and affirmations. We also explored the importance of self-awareness in accessing your inner strength and how you can use it to overcome challenges and achieve your goals.

I know that cultivating inner strength can sometimes feel like a daunting task, but remember that you already have everything you need to be strong and resilient. By using the techniques and strategies we've discussed in this chapter, you can tap into your inner strength whenever you need to and face any challenge with confidence.

But we're not done yet. In the next chapter, we're going to be talking about how to define your dreams and goals. We'll discuss how to get clear on what you truly desire and how to create a plan to make it happen. I can't wait to dive into this with you and help you start making moves towards the life you desire.

So, get ready to dream big and start making moves towards the life you desire.

3

BUILDING THE LIFE YOU DESERVE

"Nothing is impossible, the word itself says 'I'm possible'!" - Audrey Hepburn

I'm so excited to help you discover the life you deserve and define your dreams and goals. This is where the real magic happens! In this chapter, we'll be talking about how to identify your true desires, setting realistic and achievable goals, and creating a plan of action to manifest your dreams.

Let me ask you a question—what are your dreams? I'm not talking about what you think you should want, or what your parents or society tells you to want. I'm talking about what you truly desire in your heart of hearts. It's important to take the time to reflect on this and get clear on your true desires. Once you know what you really want, you can start working towards it.

Before you can manifest anything, you need to know what it is you want. That's where defining your dreams and goals comes in.

HOW TO IDENTIFY YOUR TRUE DESIRES

You are a powerful and capable woman who deserves to live the life you desire. The first step to manifesting your dreams is to define them.

What are your passions and interests?

What are the things that make you happy and light you up? What are the activities that you could do for hours without getting bored? When you explore your passions and interests, you tap into your true self and get a better understanding of what you truly desire.

What truly makes you happy?

The second thing you need to do is identify what truly makes you happy. This means reflecting on the moments in your life when you felt the happiest and most fulfilled. What were you doing, and who were you with? When you identify what truly makes you happy, you can set goals that align with those things and create a life that brings you joy and fulfillment.

What are your own desires?

Third, you need to learn to differentiate between your own desires and those imposed on you by others. As Black women, we often face pressure from society, our families, and even ourselves to pursue certain paths and goals. However, it's essential to differentiate between what we truly desire and what others want for us. When you set goals that align with your true desires, you are more likely to achieve them and feel fulfilled.

So, how do you put all of this into practice?
Here are some tips:

Start by getting clear on what you truly desire. Take some time to reflect on your passions and interests, and identify what truly makes you happy.

Write down your goals and aspirations. This helps to make them more concrete and gives you something to work towards.

Make sure your goals align with your values and passions. When your goals align with your true desires, you are more likely to achieve them and feel fulfilled.

Be open to exploring new interests and passions. Your desires and interests may change over time, so be open to exploring new things and adapting your goals accordingly.

Don't be afraid to dream big. It's okay to set ambitious goals and dream big. Remember, you are capable of achieving anything you set your mind to.

SETTING REALISTIC AND ACHIEVABLE GOALS

Let's dive into how you can define your dreams and goals, so you can start manifesting them in your life. One of the most important things to remember when defining your dreams and goals is to make sure they are realistic and achievable. This means you need to set SMART goals that are specific, measurable, achievable, relevant, and time-bound.

Setting SMART goals is so important because it gives you a clear target to aim for and a way to track your progress. You also need to break down big goals into smaller, actionable steps so that they don't feel too overwhelming or unattainable. When you have smaller steps to focus on, it's much easier to make progress and stay motivated.

However, it's important to avoid setting goals that are too lofty or unrealistic. While it's great to dream big, setting goals that are unachievable can lead to frustration, disappointment, and ultimately giving up. You need to find the right balance between pushing yourself to achieve more and setting goals that are within reach.

To help illustrate the importance of SMART goals, let me give you a real-life example. Let's say your goal is to run a marathon. Rather than just setting the goal of running a marathon, which could be overwhelming, you can break down that goal into smaller, SMART goals. For example, you could set the goal of running a 5K in 6 months, then a 10K in 8 months, a half marathon in 12 months, and finally, a marathon in 18 months.

By setting SMART goals and breaking them down into smaller, actionable steps, you can track your progress and stay motivated. When you achieve each milestone, you will feel more confident and excited to keep moving forward towards your ultimate goal.

Setting realistic and achievable goals is key to defining your dreams and making them a reality. By setting SMART goals, breaking them down into smaller steps, and avoiding goals that are too lofty, you can stay motivated and on track to achieve your dreams.

CREATING A PLAN OF ACTION TO MANIFEST YOUR DREAMS

Girl, you already know we face unique challenges in realizing our potential and achieving our goals. But, let me tell you, it's not impossible! We can manifest our dreams if we're intentional and create a plan of action that aligns with our vision.

As we journey towards manifesting our dreams, it's essential to create a plan of action to help us stay organized, focused, and on track. The plan will provide a roadmap to achieving our goals, making our dreams more meaningful, achievable, and enjoyable. Visualization is a powerful tool that can help us create an intentional plan of action that aligns with our unique needs. It allows us to see our dreams come to life in our mind's eye, helping us visualize our future selves and the steps we need to take to get there. With visualization, we can create a roadmap to our success and make our dreams a reality.

First, let's talk about the power of visualization in creating a plan of action. Visualization is a process of using your imagination to create a picture of what you want in your mind's eye. This process helps you create a mental picture of your dream life, enabling you to plan your actions in a way that is achievable, focused, and realistic. It's essential to be specific about what you want, be clear about your goals and dreams, and imagine yourself already living that life. Use your senses to create a vivid picture of what that life looks like. This process will help you create a mental roadmap of your goals, allowing you to create a plan of action that is tailored to your unique needs.

Vision Board

Another tool that can help us stay focused on our goals is a vision board. A vision board is a visual representation of your goals and dreams, which helps you stay motivated and focused on the things that matter most to you. The board can be created using images, words, or symbols that resonate with your dreams and goals. By creating a vision board, you can see your dreams come to life and use the power of visualization to create a plan of action that is tailored to your needs.

To create a vision board, you need to identify your goals and dreams. Collect images, words, or symbols that represent these goals and dreams. Arrange them on a board in a way that is visually appealing to you. You can hang the board in a place where you'll see it every day, reminding you of your goals and dreams. The vision board will serve as a reminder of the things that matter most to you, helping you stay motivated and focused on achieving your goals.

Staying accountable

Accountability helps you stay on track, reminding you of your goals and the actions you need to take to achieve them. To stay accountable, you can find an accountability partner or join a community of like-minded individuals who share your goals and dreams. These individuals will help you stay motivated, focused, and on track, providing you with the support and encouragement you need to achieve your goals.

Consistent action

Finally, taking consistent action is another critical aspect of manifesting your dreams. You need to take consistent action towards your goals, no matter how small the steps may be. These actions will build momentum and create a snowball effect, propelling you towards your dreams. By taking consistent action, you're putting your plan of action into practice, enabling you to achieve your goals and create the life you desire.

How to apply these principles in real life? Let's go over an example.

Imagine your dream is to start your own business. You can visualize yourself owning a successful business, enjoying financial freedom, and being your own boss. You can create a vision board that includes images of successful entrepreneurs, your business idea, and other relevant items that speak to you.

Next, you need to stay accountable and take consistent action towards achieving your dream. You can find a mentor or accountability partner who has experience in starting and running a successful business. They can offer advice, support, and encouragement to help you stay on track. You can also join a community of like-minded individuals who are also starting their businesses, where you can share your experiences, ask for help, and provide support to others.

To take consistent action, you can break down your big goal of starting a business into smaller, actionable steps. These steps can include researching your target market, developing a business plan, finding funding, and creating a marketing strategy. By taking consistent action towards these smaller goals, you'll build momentum and move closer to realizing your big dream of owning a successful business.

As you can see, creating a plan of action is essential when it comes to manifesting your dreams. Visualization, creating a vision board, staying accountable, and taking consistent action are all critical components of a successful plan.

SUMMARY, ACTION STEPS & EXERCISES:

- Take some time to journal about what truly makes you happy. What are some things that you enjoy doing that bring you joy and fulfillment?
- Choose one of your big goals and break it down into smaller, actionable steps. Write down each step and assign a deadline for completion.
- Create a vision board that includes images and words that represent your goals and desires. Hang it in a visible location as a reminder to stay focused on your dreams.
- Make a list of everything you want to achieve in the next year.
- Circle the top three things on your list that are most important to you.
- For each of those three things, write down three smaller goals you can achieve in the next 90 days.

How did it feel to reflect on your true desires and set achievable goals? I hope you're feeling inspired and motivated to take the next step towards manifesting your dreams.

In this chapter, we dove deep into how to define your dreams and goals. We talked about the importance of identifying your true desires and setting realistic and achievable goals. By breaking down your goals into smaller, actionable steps, you'll be able to make progress towards your dreams and stay motivated along the way.

We also explored how to create a plan of action that includes visualization, a vision board, and consistent action. By doing this, you'll be able to keep your goals front and center in your mind and take consistent steps towards making them a reality.

I know that setting goals can be daunting, but I want you to know that you have everything you need to achieve your dreams. By following the techniques and strategies we've discussed in this chapter, you'll be well on your way to living the life you truly desire.

But, as I'm sure you know, sometimes we can be held back by our own limiting beliefs. That's why in the next chapter, we'll be talking about how to overcome those beliefs and step into your true potential. I can't wait to dive into this with you and help you unleash the power within.

Are you ready to take the next step towards your dreams? Let's do this, girl!

Keep shining!

Hey girl,

I hope the book is aiding your self-empowerment journey. If so, please consider leaving a review.

Your feedback not only lets me know what resonates with you, but also helps more Black women discover the book and its transformative message.

<u>LEAVE A QUICK REVIEW</u>

US · SCAN ME · UK

Your support plays a significant role in promoting self-love and empowerment for Black women globally. Let's continue sharing the love!

With gratitude,

Jada Amari

4

BREAKING FREE FROM SELF-SABOTAGE

"Beliefs have the power to create and the power to destroy." - Tony Robbins

Girl, are you ready to tackle those limiting beliefs and step into your power? In this chapter, we're going to dive deep into identifying and challenging those beliefs that are holding you back. Trust me, we all have them. But the key to manifestation is to recognize them and reprogram your mindset to support your goals and desires.

We'll start by exploring what limiting beliefs are and how they show up in our lives. From there, we'll dive into specific techniques for reprogramming your mindset, including visualization, affirmations, and self-talk.

But the real magic happens when you shift your perspective and beliefs to support your manifestation. We'll explore how to do this by examining your core values, understanding your fears, and creating a positive, growth-oriented mindset.

By the end of this chapter, you'll have a clear understanding of your limiting beliefs and the tools to overcome them. You'll be well on your way to creating a mindset that supports your manifestation and empowers you to live the life of your dreams.

HOW MANIFESTATION CAN HELP YOU OVERCOME LIMITING BELIEFS AND CREATE THE LIFE YOU DESIRE

Limiting beliefs are those negative thoughts that hold us back from achieving our goals and living our best lives. They can come from past experiences, societal messages, or even our own self-doubt. As Black women, we often face a variety of limiting beliefs that can stifle our potential and prevent us from achieving greatness. Whether it's the belief that we don't deserve success or that we're not good enough to pursue our dreams, these thoughts can be incredibly damaging to our self-esteem and our ability to manifest the life we desire.

But here's the thing: limiting beliefs are just thoughts. They're not necessarily true, and they don't have to define us or dictate our future. In fact, by practicing the art of manifestation, we can learn to overcome these negative beliefs and create the life we truly want.

Now, this doesn't mean that you can just sit on your couch and think happy thoughts and expect everything to magically fall into place. Manifestation requires action, too. But the point is that by shifting your mindset and beliefs, you can open yourself up to new opportunities and possibilities that you might not have otherwise noticed or pursued.

So, how can manifestation help you overcome limiting beliefs and create the life you desire?

First, it's important to recognize that limiting beliefs are often deeply ingrained in our subconscious minds. We might not even be aware of them, but they can still impact our thoughts and behaviors. By practicing manifestation techniques like visualization, affirmations, and gratitude, we can begin to rewire our subconscious minds and replace negative beliefs with more positive ones.

Defining our limiting beliefs is the first step towards overcoming them. It's important to identify the negative self-talk that holds us back and replace it with positive, growth-oriented beliefs that support our manifestation practice.

Limiting beliefs can be tricky to identify because they are often deeply ingrained in our psyche. Here are a few examples of common limiting beliefs:

- "I'm not smart enough to achieve my dreams."
- "I don't have enough money to start my own business."
- "I'm not pretty enough to attract a loving partner."
- "I don't have the connections to make my dreams a reality."

These beliefs can be insidious, quietly sabotaging our efforts to manifest our dreams. However, the good news is that they can be challenged and changed with conscious effort.

Let's say you have a limiting belief that you're not good enough to start your own business. Every time you think about pursuing your dream, you feel a sense of fear and doubt creeping in. To overcome this belief, you might try visualizing yourself as a successful entrepreneur, feeling confident and capable while setting clear goals and intentions.

You could also use affirmations, like "I am capable of creating a successful business" or "I deserve to pursue my dreams." By focusing on these positive thoughts and beliefs, you'll start to shift your mindset and build more confidence in yourself and your abilities.

DIG DEEP—EXAMINE YOUR CORE VALUES, UNDERSTAND YOUR FEARS, AND CREATE A POSITIVE, GROWTH-ORIENTED MINDSET

Let me give you an example of how to examine your core values, understand your fears, and create a positive, growth-oriented mindset.

Perhaps your dream is to become a successful writer. First, take a moment to examine your core values. What matters most to you in life? Is it creativity, freedom, financial independence, or something else? Knowing your core values will help you create a manifestation practice that is authentic and meaningful to you.

Next, identify the fears that are holding you back from achieving your dream. Are you afraid of failure, rejection, or not being good enough? Once you've identified your fears, take a moment to understand why you have these fears. Is it because of past experiences, societal pressure, or self-doubt? Understanding the root cause of your fears will help you challenge them and reprogram your mindset.

Now, it's time to create a positive, growth-oriented mindset. Start by reframing your limiting beliefs into positive affirmations. For example, if you believe that you're not good enough to be a writer, reframe that belief into "I am a talented writer with a unique voice." Repeat these affirmations to yourself every day, and visualize yourself living your dream life as a successful writer.

Additionally, you can take action towards your goal by setting small, achievable goals for yourself. For instance, you can set a goal to write for 30 minutes a day or attend a writing workshop to improve your skills. Celebrate each accomplishment along the way, and don't be discouraged by setbacks.

CHALLENGING LIMITING BELIEFS

Challenging limiting beliefs is essential to your manifestation practice. Your beliefs shape your reality, so if you have limiting beliefs, they'll create limitations in your life. Challenging your limiting beliefs means questioning your thoughts, and reframing your beliefs to align with your goals and dreams. This process is necessary to shift your mindset and create a positive, growth-oriented mindset that supports your manifestation practice. By challenging your limiting beliefs, you'll break down the barriers that hold you back and unleash your true potential.

Journaling

One way to challenge limiting beliefs is through journaling. Writing down our thoughts and beliefs can help us see them more objectively and identify patterns of negative self-talk. We can then question those thoughts, asking ourselves if they are true, and if there is evidence to support them. If not, we can begin to reframe our beliefs with positive self-talk.

Question the source

Another technique for challenging limiting beliefs is to question the source of those beliefs. Where did we learn to believe these negative things about ourselves? Are they based on past experiences, societal messages, or our own insecurities? Once we understand the source of our limiting beliefs, we can begin to replace them with more positive, growth-oriented beliefs.

Reprogram the mind

Visualizations, affirmations, and self-talk are powerful tools for reprogramming our mindset and overcoming limiting beliefs. By visualizing ourselves achieving our goals and repeating positive affirmations, we can replace negative self-talk with positive, empowering beliefs. We can use self-talk to encourage ourselves and stay motivated towards achieving our goals.

When you have a specific vision for what you want to achieve, it becomes easier to stay focused and motivated, even when faced with obstacles or setbacks. By regularly visualizing your goals and taking action towards them, you'll start to build momentum and create a sense of progress and accomplishment.

Of course, there will still be challenges and setbacks along the way. But by using manifestation techniques to cultivate a positive and resilient mindset, you'll be better equipped to handle whatever comes your way. You'll be able to recognize your own strength and worth, and to stay focused on your goals even when things get tough.

POWERFUL VISUALIZATIONS, AFFIRMATIONS, AND POSITIVE SELF-TALK

Below are a variety of visualizations, affirmations, and positive self-talk to help you reprogram your mindset. The best part? You can customize them to fit your unique needs and goals. And to make it even easier for you, I've grouped them into different categories so you can incorporate them into your daily routine seamlessly.

Self-Love and Self-Acceptance

- "I love and accept myself exactly as I am."
- "I am worthy of love, success, and happiness."
- "I choose to see myself through the lens of compassion and kindness."

Abundance and Prosperity

- "I attract abundance and prosperity into my life effortlessly."
- "I am deserving of wealth and financial freedom."
- "Money flows to me easily and effortlessly."

Health and Wellness

- "I am strong, healthy, and full of energy."
- "My body is a temple, and I treat it with love and respect."
- "I make healthy choices that nourish my mind, body, and soul."

Career and Business

- "I am confident in my skills and abilities, and I am open to new opportunities."
- "I am successful in my career/business, and I am constantly growing and learning."
- "My work is fulfilling, and I am making a positive impact in the world."

Relationships and Connection

- "I attract positive and uplifting relationships into my life."
- "I am surrounded by people who love and support me."
- "I am worthy of healthy and loving relationships, and I communicate my needs with ease."

It's essential to identify your negative self-talk patterns, question their validity, and replace them with more positive and realistic thoughts. And don't forget about the power of positive affirmations! These simple statements can have a profound impact on your inner dialogue and self-esteem.

So what are you waiting for? Start incorporating these techniques into your daily routine and watch as your mindset shifts towards positivity and empowerment.

SUMMARY, ACTION STEPS & EXERCISES:

- Identify and challenge one of your limiting beliefs.
- Create a visualization or affirmation that supports your manifestation.
- Reflect on your core values and how they relate to your manifestation practice.
- Write down one fear that is holding you back and one action you can take to overcome it.

* * *

I hope you're feeling empowered and ready to take on the world after reading this chapter. We just covered a whole lot of ground, but let me give you a quick summary to make sure it all sinks in.

We started by exploring what limiting beliefs are and how they can hold you back from manifesting the life you truly desire. Then, we talked about the importance of recognizing and challenging those beliefs. We dove into the specific techniques you can use to reprogram your mindset, such as visualization, affirmations, and self-talk.

But that's not all—we also talked about how to shift your perspective and beliefs to support your manifestation goals. By examining your core values, understanding your fears, and creating a positive, growth-oriented mindset, you'll be well on your way to living the life of your dreams.

I know that it can be tough to overcome limiting beliefs, but I want you to know that you have the power to do it. By using the techniques and strategies we've discussed in this chapter, you'll be well on your way to creating a mindset that supports your manifestation.

But we're not done yet, girlfriend! The next chapter is all about cultivating self-awareness and connecting with your true desires. You'll learn how to get in touch with your authentic self and identify what you truly want in life. Trust me, this is where the real magic happens.

So, take a moment to reflect on what you've learned in this chapter and start putting it into practice. Remember, manifestation is a practice, and it takes time and dedication to see results. But with the right mindset and techniques, you can achieve anything you set your mind to.

Are you ready to take the next step on your manifestation journey? I can't wait to see what you'll achieve. Let's dive into the next chapter and discover how to connect with your true desires.

5

THE KEY TO UNLOCKING YOUR BEST SELF

"Owning our story and loving ourselves through that process is the bravest thing that we'll ever do." - Brené Brown

*H*ey gorgeous, I'm thrilled to dive into Chapter 5 with you! Cultivating self-awareness is a crucial part of manifesting the life you've always dreamed of. It's about going beyond surface-level understanding and developing a deep, intimate relationship with yourself. Self-awareness empowers you to recognize and address the negative thought patterns and behaviors that are holding you back from your full potential.

In this chapter, we'll explore the importance of self-reflection and introspection as powerful tools to gain a deeper understanding of yourself. We'll also delve into techniques for developing self-awareness, including meditation, journaling, and mindfulness practices. With these tools, you'll be able to identify your limiting beliefs, emotional triggers, and patterns of behavior that may be holding you back from reaching your manifestation goals.

You'll learn how to use self-awareness to align with your manifestation goals by setting intentions, practicing gratitude, and visualizing your ideal life. By the end of this chapter, you'll have a deeper understanding of yourself and how to use self-awareness as a powerful tool for manifesting the life of your dreams.

Let's do this!

THE IMPORTANCE OF SELF-REFLECTION AND INTROSPECTION

Self-reflection is the process of looking within yourself and examining your thoughts, feelings, and behaviors. It's a time for introspection, where you can delve deep into your innermost thoughts and feelings. Taking time for self-reflection is essential for personal growth. By examining our thoughts and emotions, we can better understand our beliefs and behaviors, identify limiting beliefs and patterns that are holding us back, and make conscious choices that support our goals.

Self-reflection and introspection are powerful tools for personal growth. These practices require us to take a step back from our daily lives and ask ourselves important questions about who we are, what we want, and where we're going.

WHY TAKING TIME FOR SELF-REFLECTION IS IMPORTANT FOR PERSONAL GROWTH

Taking time for self-reflection is crucial for personal growth because it allows us to identify our strengths and weaknesses, our values, and our goals. When we take the time to reflect on our lives, we become more aware of who we are and what we want, enabling us to make better decisions and take more meaningful actions towards our goals.

Self-reflection also helps us to identify patterns of behavior that may be holding us back. These patterns can be in the form of limiting beliefs, negative self-talk, or fear-based actions. By identifying these patterns, we can take steps to break free from them and create a more positive, growth-oriented mindset.

To cultivate self-awareness, you need to set aside time to reflect on your life. You can do this by taking a walk in nature, writing in a journal, or meditating. It's essential to create a quiet, distraction-free environment that allows you to focus on your thoughts and emotions.

During this time of reflection, you can ask yourself important questions, such as:

- What are my values?
- What are my goals?
- What are my strengths and weaknesses?
- What patterns of behavior am I repeating?
- What limiting beliefs do I have that are holding me back?
- What actions can I take to create a more positive, growth-oriented mindset?

By asking yourself these questions, you're taking the first step towards cultivating self-awareness, which is an essential aspect of personal growth.

HOW TO CREATE SPACE FOR INTROSPECTION IN YOUR DAILY LIFE

Creating space for introspection in your daily life can be challenging, especially when we're constantly bombarded with distractions and demands on our time. However, setting aside time for introspection is crucial for personal growth and achieving your goals. Here are some tips to help you create space for introspection in your daily life:

- **Start small:** carving out even five minutes a day for self-reflection can make a big difference in your life. Over time, you can gradually increase the amount of time you spend on introspection.

- **Schedule it:** Set aside a specific time each day for introspection. Make it a non-negotiable part of your routine.
- **Disconnect:** Turn off your phone and other electronic devices. Find a quiet space where you can be alone with your thoughts.
- **Write it down:** Journaling can be a powerful tool for introspection. Write down your thoughts, feelings, and insights as you reflect on your life and goals.

THE BENEFITS OF DEVELOPING A DEEPER UNDERSTANDING OF YOURSELF

In life, it's easy to get caught up in the day-to-day hustle and forget about ourselves. We're often so busy trying to keep up with work, family, and friends that we forget to take time for ourselves. It's essential to develop a deeper understanding of ourselves to live a happier, more fulfilled life.

Taking the time to reflect on who we are and what we want from life can help us cultivate greater self-awareness. Self-awareness is a critical component of personal growth, and it helps us live life more intentionally.

By developing a deeper understanding of ourselves, we can achieve the following benefits:

1. **Improved decision-making:** When we understand our values, beliefs, and desires, we can make better decisions that align with our true selves. This leads to more fulfillment and happiness in life.
2. **Greater self-confidence:** When we understand ourselves better, we have a clearer sense of who we are and what we stand for. This clarity leads to greater self-

confidence, and we can move through life with more ease and grace.

3. **Increased resilience:** When we understand ourselves better, we can weather life's challenges with greater ease. We can bounce back from setbacks and challenges because we know who we are and what we're capable of.

4. **Better relationships:** When we understand ourselves better, we can form deeper connections with others. We can communicate more effectively, be more empathetic, and form more meaningful relationships.

So, why is it essential to take the time to develop a deeper understanding of yourself? Because doing so will help you lead a happier, more fulfilled life. It will help you make better decisions, have greater self-confidence, be more resilient, and form deeper relationships.

One way to develop greater self-awareness is to take the time for self-reflection. This means taking the time to reflect on who you are, what you believe in, and what you want from life. It's about getting in touch with your emotions, desires, and needs. You can do this by journaling, meditating, or talking to a trusted friend or therapist.

Another way to develop greater self-awareness is to explore your values and beliefs. What's important to you? What do you believe in? What are your non-negotiables? By understanding your values and beliefs, you can make decisions that align with your true self.

Developing a deeper understanding of yourself is critical to personal growth and living a more fulfilled life. It can lead to improved decision-making, greater self-confidence, increased resilience, and better relationships. So take the time to reflect on who you are and what you want from life. You'll be glad you did!

TECHNIQUES FOR DEVELOPING SELF-AWARENESS

Let's explore some meditation and mindfulness practices, journaling and self-inquiry techniques, and seeking feedback from others to gain a new perspective.

Meditation and mindfulness practices for developing self-awareness

Meditation and mindfulness practices are powerful tools that can help you develop self-awareness. These practices involve focusing your attention on the present moment, allowing you to become more aware of your thoughts, feelings, and sensations.

To begin, find a quiet and comfortable space where you won't be disturbed. Sit comfortably with your back straight and close your eyes. Begin to focus on your breath, noticing the sensation of the air moving in and out of your body. If your mind begins to wander, gently bring your attention back to your breath.

Another mindfulness practice is to focus on your senses, paying attention to the world around you. Notice the sounds you can hear, the sensations you can feel, and the smells you can detect. This practice can help you become more aware of the present moment, allowing you to gain insight into your thoughts, feelings, and actions.

Journaling and self-inquiry techniques for gaining insight into your thoughts and feelings

Journaling and self-inquiry techniques are powerful tools that can help you gain insight into your thoughts and feelings. These practices involve reflecting on your experiences, allowing you to become more aware of your emotions and behaviors.

To begin, find a quiet and comfortable space where you won't be disturbed. Grab a journal and a pen and begin to reflect on your experiences. Ask yourself questions like:

- How do I feel right now?
- What are my current thoughts and emotions?
- What are my goals and aspirations?
- What are my fears and worries?
- What are my strengths and weaknesses?

Answering these questions can help you gain insight into your thoughts and feelings, enabling you to create a more meaningful and fulfilling life.

Seeking feedback from others to gain a new perspective

Seeking feedback from others is a powerful tool that can help you gain a new perspective on your thoughts, feelings, and actions. Other people can provide you with valuable insights and feedback that you may not have considered on your own.

To begin, identify someone you trust and respect who can provide you with honest feedback. Ask them to share their thoughts on your thoughts, feelings, and actions, and be open to receiving constructive criticism. This feedback can help you gain insight into your blind spots and identify areas for growth and development.

Self-awareness is a powerful tool that can help you gain insight into your thoughts, feelings, and actions, enabling you to create a more meaningful and fulfilling life. These techniques for developing self-awareness can help you cultivate a more mindful and intentional life, allowing you to achieve your goals and dreams.

SELF-AWARENESS TO ALIGN WITH YOUR MANIFESTATION GOALS

As you journey towards manifesting your goals, it's essential to use self-awareness to align your thoughts, emotions, and actions. When you're in alignment with your desires, you can easily attract and manifest what you want.

To start, let's talk about how self-awareness can help you align with your manifestation goals. Self-awareness involves understanding your thoughts, feelings, and behaviors and how they affect your life. By being self-aware, you can identify any negative thought patterns or behaviors that are blocking you from manifesting your desires.

One way to use self-awareness to align with your manifestation goals is to regularly check in with yourself and reflect on your thoughts and emotions. Take a few minutes each day to meditate, journal, or simply sit in silence and observe your thoughts. Notice any negative thoughts or limiting beliefs that arise and write them down. This will help you become aware of any patterns or behaviors that are holding you back.

Next, it's essential to identify and change limiting beliefs and behaviors that are holding you back from manifesting your goals. Limiting beliefs are negative thoughts or beliefs that hold you back from achieving your goals. Examples of limiting beliefs include "I'm not good enough," "I don't deserve success," or "I'll never be able to achieve my dreams."

To change these beliefs, start by identifying them and questioning their validity. Ask yourself if these beliefs are true, and if not, replace them with positive affirmations. For example, if you believe that you're not good enough, replace that belief with "I am capable and deserving of success." Over time, these positive affirmations will help you cultivate a growth mindset and positive self-talk.

Speaking of a growth mindset and positive self-talk, it's essential to cultivate these to stay aligned with your manifestation goals. A growth mindset is a belief that your abilities and intelligence can be developed through dedication and hard work. Positive self-talk involves replacing negative thoughts with positive ones. Both of these practices can help you stay focused on your goals and maintain a positive attitude.

To cultivate a growth mindset, focus on your strengths and successes rather than your failures. When you encounter obstacles, view them as opportunities to learn and grow. When it comes to positive self-talk, use affirmations that align with your manifestation goals. For example, if you're manifesting abundance, use affirmations such as "I am worthy of abundance and prosperity."

Finally, staying aligned with your manifestation goals requires regular self-awareness practices. Make it a habit to check in with yourself daily, reflect on your thoughts and emotions, and adjust your actions accordingly. Practice gratitude for the things you have manifested, and visualize yourself already living the life you desire.

By using self-awareness to align with your manifestation goals, identifying and changing limiting beliefs and behaviors, cultivating a growth mindset and positive self-talk, and staying aligned with your manifestation goals through self-awareness practices, you can manifest the life of your dreams. Remember, you have the power to create the life you want, and by using these practices consistently, you can achieve anything you desire.

SUMMARY, ACTION STEPS & EXERCISES:

- Take 10 minutes each day for self-reflection and introspection.
- Start a journal and use prompts to gain insight into your thoughts and feelings.
- Ask a trusted friend or mentor for feedback on a specific area of your life.
- Identify one limiting belief or behavior that is holding you back and work on changing it.

Hey sis, great job on making it through Chapter 5! In this chapter, we talked about the importance of cultivating self-awareness and how it can help you align with your manifestation goals. We explored some practical techniques for developing self-awareness, including mindfulness, self-reflection, and journaling. We also talked about how to use self-awareness to identify limiting beliefs and patterns that might be holding you back from manifesting your dreams.

One thing we talked about in Chapter 5 is how easy it can be to get stuck in patterns of thought and behavior that don't serve us. Without self-awareness, we might not even realize that we're repeating the same mistakes or falling into the same negative thought patterns.

But when we cultivate self-awareness, we can start to notice these patterns and make changes. You can make more conscious choices and take actions that align with your values and desires.

Self-awareness is all about understanding who you are, what you want, and what might be standing in the way of achieving your goals.

So, what's next? In the next chapter, we'll be talking about the power of gratitude. Gratitude is a simple yet powerful practice that can help you shift your mindset and attract more abundance and joy into your life. We'll be discussing different techniques for practicing gratitude and how it can help you on your manifestation journey.

I can't wait to share more with you about this, so let's dive in and start harnessing the power of gratitude together!

Keep up the good work!

6

ONE DAILY HABIT FOR
TRANSFORMING YOUR LIFE

"Gratitude unlocks the fullness of life. It turns what we have into enough, and more. It turns denial into acceptance, chaos to order, confusion to clarity. It can turn a meal into a feast, a house into a home, a stranger into a friend." - Melody Beattie

*A*re you ready to tap into the power of gratitude and accelerate your manifestation process? In this chapter, we'll be diving into the incredible benefits of gratitude, and how it can transform your life.

We'll explore different techniques for cultivating gratitude and show you how to use it to manifest your deepest desires. You'll discover how practicing gratitude can shift your mindset and attract more abundance, joy, and positivity into your life.

By the end of this chapter, you'll have a deeper understanding of how gratitude can enhance your life and elevate your manifestation game. You'll have practical tools and exercises to incorporate a gratitude practice into your daily routine and create a positive shift in your life.

Are you ready to unlock the power of gratitude and experience more abundance and joy in your life? Let's do this, sis!

BENEFITS OF A GRATITUDE PRACTICE

Gratitude is a simple yet transformative practice that can help you cultivate a positive mindset and align your thoughts and emotions with your goals.

Practicing gratitude can help you shift your focus from what's wrong to what's right in your life. It can help you feel more positive and uplifted, no matter what challenges you may be facing. So, let's dive into the benefits of a gratitude practice.

- **Cultivates a positive mindset**

One of the most significant benefits of a gratitude practice is that it helps cultivate a positive mindset. When you focus on the good things in your life, you're training your brain to see the positive, even in difficult situations. This can help you feel more optimistic and hopeful, which can have a positive impact on your mental health and well-being.

- **Increases feelings of happiness and contentment**

When you practice gratitude regularly, you'll likely notice that you feel happier and more content with your life. Focusing on the things you're grateful for can bring a sense of joy and fulfillment that can be hard to find when you're constantly focused on what's wrong. Gratitude can help you feel more connected to the present moment and to the people and things that matter most to you.

Reduces stress and anxiety

Another benefit of a gratitude practice is that it can help reduce stress and anxiety. When you're focused on what you're grateful for, you're less likely to get caught up in negative thinking and worry. This can help you feel more relaxed and at ease, which can be especially helpful during challenging times.

- **Improves relationships**

Gratitude can also improve your relationships with others. When you're focused on what you appreciate about the people in your life, you're more likely to treat them with kindness and respect. This can help strengthen your relationships and create a more positive, supportive environment for everyone involved.

- **Boosts physical health**

Did you know? Practicing gratitude can even have physical health benefits. Studies have shown that people who practice gratitude regularly have lower blood pressure, better immune function, and better sleep. When you feel more positive and relaxed, your body can function more optimally, leading to better overall health.

Gratitude is an essential ingredient in manifesting your dreams. It helps you shift your focus from what you lack to what you have, enabling you to appreciate the abundance you already have in your life and attract more positivity and more abundance.

HOW GRATITUDE AFFECTS THE BRAIN AND PROMOTES POSITIVITY

Gratitude is not just a feel-good practice; it also has a physiological impact on the brain. Gratitude can promote positive emotions and thoughts, leading to improved well-being and mental health. Research has shown that practicing gratitude can:

- Increase dopamine and serotonin levels, which are neurotransmitters associated with pleasure and happiness
- Activate the hypothalamus, which regulates stress levels and sleep patterns
- Boost activity in the prefrontal cortex, which is responsible for decision-making, attention, and emotional regulation
- Improve neural pathways that are associated with empathy and social cognition

These changes in the brain can lead to improved well-being, reduced symptoms of depression and anxiety, and a more positive outlook on life.

TECHNIQUES FOR CULTIVATING GRATITUDE

Now that you understand the benefits of a gratitude practice and how it affects the brain, let's explore some techniques for cultivating gratitude in your life.

Gratitude journaling

Gratitude journaling is a powerful technique that can help you cultivate a positive mindset and shift your focus from what you lack to what you have. To start, set aside some time each day to write down three things that you are grateful for. These can be small things like a delicious cup of coffee or big things like a loving family or a fulfilling job. By focusing on the good in your life, you'll begin to notice more things to be grateful for and attract more positivity into your life.

Daily affirmations

Using affirmations is a powerful way to reprogram your mindset and align your thoughts and emotions with your goals. Affirmations help you stay positive and focused on the things that matter most to you. When you add gratitude to your affirmations, you're cultivating a mindset of abundance, and that can help you manifest your desires more quickly.

Here are ten examples of gratitude affirmations that you can use every day to stay motivated, focused, and grateful:

1. I am grateful for all the blessings in my life, and I know that more are on the way.
2. I am thankful for my health, my loved ones, and the abundance that surrounds me every day.
3. I appreciate the challenges in my life, as they have helped me grow and become a better person.
4. I am grateful for the opportunities that come my way, and I am ready to embrace them fully.
5. I am thankful for my talents and abilities, and I know they will help me achieve my dreams.
6. I appreciate the beauty in nature, and I am thankful for the joy and peace it brings me.
7. I am grateful for the people in my life who support me, love me, and inspire me to be my best self.
8. I am thankful for the lessons I have learned, and I know they will help me in my future endeavors.
9. I appreciate the simple pleasures in life, such as laughter, sunshine, and a good book.
10. I am grateful for this moment right now, and I know that it is the only moment that truly matters.

Repeat these affirmations to yourself each day, and you'll begin to cultivate a more positive mindset and attract more abundance into your life.

Expressing gratitude to others

Expressing gratitude to others is a powerful way to cultivate gratitude and improve your relationships with others. Take time each day to express gratitude to someone in your life, whether it's a friend, family member, or coworker. Let them know how much you appreciate them and how they have impacted your life in a positive way. By expressing gratitude to others, you'll not only cultivate more gratitude in your own life but also spread positivity and kindness to those around you.

ACCELERATE YOUR MANIFESTATION PROCESS WITH GRATITUDE

As we journey towards manifesting our dreams, we must be intentional about aligning our thoughts and emotions with our goals. Gratitude is a powerful tool that can accelerate your manifestation process by helping you align your thoughts and emotions with your goals. When you cultivate gratitude, you shift your focus from what you lack to what you have, which can help you attract more positivity and abundance into your life. Gratitude can help you feel more aligned with your goals, making it easier to visualize them and take action towards achieving them.

When you practice gratitude, you attract more positive energy into your life, which can help you manifest your desires more easily. When you're in a state of gratitude, you're more likely to notice opportunities and take action towards your goals. Gratitude can help you stay focused on your goals and remain optimistic even when facing obstacles and challenges.

Here are some ways to use gratitude to align your thoughts and emotions with your goals:

Recognize the Good Things in Your Life

The first step to practicing gratitude is to recognize the good things in your life. Take a few moments each day to reflect on the things you're thankful for. It could be something as simple as having a roof over your head or having a supportive friend. By acknowledging the good things in your life, you're cultivating a mindset of abundance and positivity that can help you attract more of what you want.

Visualize Your Desired Outcome

After recognizing the good things in your life, the next step is to visualize your desired outcome. Imagine yourself already living the life you desire. What does it look like? How does it feel? What emotions are you experiencing? By focusing on the positive aspects of your desired outcome, you're aligning your thoughts and emotions with your goals. This can help you manifest your desires more quickly and easily. In the next chapter we will do a deep dive on visualizing techniques to help you achieve your best life.

Express Gratitude for Your Desired Outcome

The next step is to express gratitude for your desired outcome. Even if you haven't achieved your goal yet, express gratitude as if you already have. For example, if your goal is to start a successful business, express gratitude for the business as if it already exists. By expressing gratitude in this way, you're sending a signal to the universe that you're ready to receive what you desire.

Practice Gratitude Daily

Finally, it's essential to practice gratitude daily. Make it a part of your daily routine to acknowledge the good things in your life, visualize your desired outcome, and express gratitude for what you want. This can be as simple as writing down what you're grateful for in a journal, meditating on your desired outcome, or simply taking a few moments to reflect on the positive aspects of your life. By making gratitude a daily practice, you're aligning your thoughts and emotions with your goals.

By aligning your thoughts and emotions with your goals, you can manifest them more quickly and easily. The universe responds to the energy that you put out, so by cultivating gratitude, you attract more positivity and abundance into your life, which can help you manifest your desires.

SUMMARY, ACTION STEPS & EXERCISES:

- Start a gratitude journal and write down three things you're grateful for each day.
- Practice daily affirmations that express gratitude for the good things in your life.
- Express gratitude to at least one person each day.
- Take a moment each day to visualize your goals and express gratitude for them as if they've already come true.

* * *

Hey sis, I hope you're feeling good and grateful today! Chapter 6 was all about harnessing the power of gratitude, and I hope you learned a lot about how a gratitude practice can transform your life. We talked about the benefits of gratitude, techniques for cultivating gratitude, and how gratitude can accelerate your manifestation process.

One of the biggest takeaways from this chapter is that gratitude is a powerful tool that can help you create more abundance and positivity in your life. When you practice gratitude, you shift your focus from what you don't have to what you do have, and that can create a sense of contentment and peace that is truly transformative.

We also talked about some practical techniques for cultivating gratitude, like keeping a gratitude journal, expressing gratitude to others, and focusing on the positive aspects of challenging situations.

By harnessing the power of gratitude, you can create a mindset of abundance and positivity that will help you manifest your dreams even faster. When you are in a state of gratitude, you are more open to receiving the things you want in life, and that can help you manifest your desires more quickly and easily.

CONCLUSION

"When you have a dream, you've got to grab it and never let go." - Carol Burnett

It's time to stop holding back and start living the life you truly desire. This book has been all about guiding you through the art of manifestation so that you can tap into your inner power, define your dreams and goals, and bring them to life. It's been a pleasure taking this journey with you, and I want to make sure that you don't just close this book and forget about it. It's time to take action!

Throughout this book, we've covered so much ground. We've talked about the principles of manifestation and how they apply to Black women, the power of mindset and intention, and the importance of tapping into your inner strength. We've talked about how to identify your true desires and create a plan of action to achieve them. We've discussed the role of self-awareness and gratitude in manifesting the life you truly desire.

So, let's take a moment to reflect on your manifestation journey. Think about where you were when you started this book and where you are now. How have you grown? What goals have you achieved? What challenges have you overcome? Celebrate yourself, sis. You've put in the work, and you deserve to acknowledge your progress.

Now, it's time to take that progress and turn it into action. It's time to put what you've learned into practice and manifest the life you truly desire. Don't let the fear of failure or the unknown hold you back. Remember that you have the power within you to make your dreams a reality. You have the power to define your own path and create the life you truly desire.

It can be difficult to let go of control and surrender to the unknown, but it's essential to the manifestation process. You don't have to do it all alone. The universe has your back, and it's ready to help you make your dreams a reality. Trust in the process and know that everything is working out for your highest good.

Remember, manifestation is a practice. It's something that you have to work at consistently. Don't give up if you don't see results right away. Keep putting in the work and trust that the universe will bring you what you desire in the right time and in the right way.

I want you to take everything you've learned in this book and apply it to your life. Create a plan of action that aligns with your goals and put it into practice. Use the techniques and strategies that we've discussed to cultivate a manifestation practice that works for you. And, most importantly, keep showing up for yourself. Keep tapping into your inner power and trusting the universe.

You've learned how to connect with your inner strength, define your dreams and goals, and overcome limiting beliefs. You've discovered the importance of self-awareness, gratitude, visualization, and self-care.

Now, it's time to start living your dreams and embracing your true potential. The manifestation journey is not a one-time event, but rather a lifelong practice. The key is to continue cultivating and strengthening your manifestation practice each day, week, and year.

So, where do you go from here? The first step is to take some time to reflect on your manifestation journey so far. Think about how far you've come, the challenges you've overcome, and the progress you've made. Take a moment to celebrate your achievements and acknowledge your hard work.

Use the techniques and tools you've learned throughout this book to create a plan of action that will help you manifest your desires. Remember to set realistic and achievable goals, and to take inspired action that aligns with your manifestation goals.

As you embark on this next chapter of your manifestation journey, remember to continue cultivating and strengthening your manifestation practice. Remember to prioritize self-care, cultivate gratitude, and surround yourself with a supportive network.

In the words of Maya Angelou, "I can be changed by what happens to me. But I refuse to be reduced by it." You have the power to create the life you desire, and the strength to overcome any obstacle in your path. Embrace your true potential and live your dreams, sis. The universe is waiting for you to manifest your greatness.

Thank you for joining me on this manifestation journey, girl. It's been a pleasure to share my personal experiences and the tools and techniques that have helped me manifest my dreams. Remember to continue cultivating and strengthening your manifestation practice, and to celebrate your progress along the way.

I want to end this book with a short story. Once upon a time, there was a woman named Sarah. Sarah had big dreams, but she didn't know how to make them a reality. She stumbled upon a book about manifestation, and she started to put what she learned into practice. She worked on her mindset, defined her goals, and took inspired action. It wasn't always easy, but she kept showing up for herself. And eventually, her dreams started to come true. She landed her dream job, found her soulmate, and started living the life she always imagined.

The best part? She realized that she had the power all along. She just needed the tools and techniques to access it.

So, what are you waiting for? It's time to take action and start living your dreams. The universe is waiting for you to embrace your true potential.

Keep shining, sis, and remember that the power to manifest your dreams is already within you. Trust yourself, trust the universe, and take inspired action towards the life you truly desire.

I am so honored to have shared this journey with you and I can't wait to see all the amazing things you will accomplish.

Go out there and live your dreams, you got this!

With love and light,

Jada Amari

REFERENCES

Alexander, J. L., & Brown, T. N. (2010). "I am not my hair": African American women and their struggles with beauty, body image, and hair. NWSA Journal, 22(2), 67-88.

Brown, M. L. (2016). Reclaiming Black beauty: A grounded theory of Black women's self-care and well-being practices. Journal of Black Psychology, 42(4), 325-354.

Bynum, M. S., & Burton, E. T. (2018). Self-care in Black women's lived experiences of depression: A phenomenological inquiry. Journal of Counseling Psychology, 65(3), 352-361.

Butler, M. (2019). Black women and mental health: An overview and call to action. Counseling Today, 61(8), 26-31.

Centers for Disease Control and Prevention. (2018). Mental health and African Americans. Retrieved from https://www.cdc.gov/vitalsigns/aahealth/mental.html

Charmaraman, L., Grossman, J. M., & Erkut, S. (2015). Mental health and gender roles in a community sample of African American and Latino adults. Psychology of Women Quarterly, 39(3), 337-349.

Clark, L. T., Watkins, L., & Piña, I. L. (2014). Elucidating the social determinants of cardiovascular disease in women: Proceedings from the Women's Health Initiative Social Determinants of Health Workshop. Circulation: Cardiovascular Quality and Outcomes, 7(5), 788-792.

Collado, H., Yoon, A. J., & Thompson, E. (2018). Culturally sensitive self-care practices for the mental health and well-being of Black women. Journal of Humanistic Psychology, 58(2), 188-208.

Doutrich, D., & Smith, T. (2019). "I have learned to love myself just as I am": Using creative writing to promote self-care and self-love among Black women. Journal of Creativity in Mental Health, 14(2), 183-196.

Fields, B. D., & Kafescioglu, N. (2017). "You are not alone": Examining the protective function of the Black church in promoting mental health and social support for Black women. Journal of Black Psychology, 43(3), 215-232.

Forbes, M. K., Eaton, N. R., & Krueger, R. F. (2019). Sexual orientation and mental health among Black, Latino, and Asian adults in the United States. Journal of Consulting and Clinical Psychology, 87(9), 815-826.

REFERENCES

Frazier, K. (2019). How to practice self-care like a Black woman. Essence. Retrieved from https://www.essence.com/lifestyle/self-care-black-women/

Grady, K. L., & Weaver, M. T. (2019). Staying sane: The challenge of promoting mental health for Black women in America. Social Work in Public Health, 34(1), 1-12.

Hartmann, W. E., Wendt, D. C., Saftner, M. A., & Marcus, M. T. (2014). Posttraumatic growth following a collective trauma: A test of socio-ecological and social identity theories. Journal of Trauma & Dissociation, 15(1), 11-28.